# Office Politics for Managers

## 90 Minute Guides

Michelle N. Halsey

Silver City Publications & Training, L.L.C.
P.O. Box 1914
Nampa, ID 83653
https://www.silvercitypublications.com/shop/

ISBN-10: 1-64004-030-7
ISBN-13: 978-1-64004-030-4

# Contents

# Chapter 1 – New Hires

Office politics, or work politics, are the strategies and procedures that employees use to function and advance in a work setting. It is important for managers to learn and understand the office environment and the employees that make it tick. Since the manager interacts with several aspects of the workplace, one should learn how to effectively work with colleagues, supervisors, and upper management in order to help keep the department functioning as a whole.

To effectively deal with office politics, you must first accept the reality that they exist in every environment. Once accepted, the manager can learn the different ways to successfully manage employees as well as build the support they need to grow.

- Understand the purpose and benefits of office politics.

- Setting boundaries and ground rules for new employees.

- Learn to interact and influence among colleagues.

- Learn how to manage various personality types in the office.

- Determine how to gain support and effectively network.

- Recognize how you are a part of a group and how you function.

**New Hires**

Once new employees are brought onboard, they are often given vital information and skills needed to succeed in the group. While this information can help them get started, the new hire will need to learn the inner workings of the office and the environment they are now a part of in order to thrive and be successful. As a manager, you can help new employees realize how the office functions and what they can do to fit right in.

## Company Core Values

Learning a company's core values is a common first step during an employee's first orientation. Having this information allows the employee to build a base knowledge of the company and how it works. Some important points to include are:

- What the core values are.

- How these values are enacted.

- What kind of results and productivity are valued.

## Building Relationships

Building key relationships with new hires ensures they will feel confident in what they do in the office and that they can come to you if they need assistance. Establishing a connection from the beginning and throughout the duration of the person's stay with the company helps them to establish their own ground while learning the politics of their environment.

Keys to building better relationships among employees:

- Create self-awareness: Identify how you appear to others.

- Establish roles as manager and employee.

- Encourage communication between colleagues as well as management (i.e. open door policy).

**Encourage Respect**

As a manager, it is important to encourage respect and etiquette among employees. Not only should you respect your workers, but respect from them is just as crucial. Any new hire is especially encouraged to respect their new coworkers and managers and establish a relationship from the beginning. An equal amount of respect should be shown to each employee and etiquette guidelines should be established.

Respect includes consideration for:

- Other people's privacy

- Employee's physical space and belongings

- Different viewpoints

- Philosophies and beliefs

- Personality

**Setting Ground Rules**

When a new employee is hired, they are expected to come into the workplace and learn to work with peers and contribute to the team. Setting ground rules before they are released to the group is a key step to ensuring they can work with others while knowing what is, or isn't, expected of them. While most of this information can be found in an employee manual or handbook, a review from the manager can make the information easily accepted and allows for any questions that may arise.

Ground rules should touch on various topics of the office, including:

- Dress code and attire

- Behavior and tolerance

- Chain of command (i.e. for complaints, questions, etc.)

- Productivity guidelines (i.e. deadlines, processes, quotas)

**It's About Interacting and Influencing**

As stated before, office politics exist in every office environment. Offices are normally made up of a wide range of people and personality types. They key to maintaining good politics is to know how to interact with each other and influence the employees under your management.

## Dealing with Different Personalities

Good relationships among employees can build the base for a better team. Different personalities have different strengths and weaknesses, which can be paired together to complement each other. Knowing the different types of personalities and how to deal with them can make any office situation easy to manage. You'll learn more about types of personalities in modules five and six.

Common office personality types:

- Complainer

- Gossiper

- Bully

- Negative Ned/Nancy

- Information Keeper

- Know-it-all

- The Apple Polisher

- Nosey Neighbor

**Build a Culture of Collaboration**

When companies grow, the group culture grows and cliques can begin to form. With so many conflicting visions, a company can lose sight of its original purpose. The goal for a manager is to form a collaboration that features every person's talents and visions.

Tips:

- Listen and observe your employees

- Be diplomatic

- Keep private matters private

- Don't get emotional – keep a professional standing

**Be Nice to Everyone (Not Just Those Who Can Help You)**

It's important to be nice to everyone in the office. As a manager, people should feel free to approach you with their problems or concerns. If they feel as though you've picked favorites or excluded others, it could not only affect their performance on the job, but yours as well. Treating everyone equally is the best way to help prevent cliques and out casting in the office.

Useful Tips:

- Stay neutral

- Don't get involved in office gossip or hype

- Watch for red flags among employees

- Monitor how you approach employees and delegate tasks

## Be a Team Player

A team player believes that they can (or the group can) get ahead by working hard and participating toward advancing the goals of the team. They know to put the team's needs ahead of their personal needs and usually follow the path needed to get the job done right the first time. As a manager, you are an important part of the team and an influential team member. Following our previous exercises, we've learned it's important to identify your team's differences and similarities in order to have the team run not only smoothly, but successfully.

Characteristics of being a team player:

- Do not make pre-judgments about your team members. Base your observations on their current work habits and behaviors.

- Provide encouragement and motivation to your employees.

- Show empathy for another worker's problems or needs.

- Keep an open mind about every member. Respect their values and opinions.

- If problems should arise with an employee or among the team, take care of it right away. Allowing them to go unsettled can cause problems among the team.

# Chapter 2 – Dealing with Rumors, Gossip, and Half-Truths

While every manager likes to believe everyone in their office gets along, unfortunately, this is not always the case. When people come together, problems such as rumors and gossip can arise and spread quickly. If these issues are not addressed and resolved from the start, they can grow larger and cause disruptions among coworkers. You have the ability to instill confidence and trust with your employees.

**Its Effects on Morale**

Although office conflicts are normal, frequent gossip, rumors or even informal comments can demoralize any employee. Negative comments that spread throughout the office cannot only be hurtful, but can cause doubt and fear among employees and affect their job performance. Employees can start to fear coming to work, question their job security, or simply make them withdraw from the group. In turn, the morale of the group drops and the team no longer works together.

**Reinforce the Truth with Facts**

When a piece of gossip or a rumor is heard in the office, our first instinct should be to stop it from spreading any further. One of the best ways to accomplish this is by discrediting the information and reinforcing the truth with the facts. Since gossip is often started through a lack of communication or a lack of knowledge, a little education or open communication can go a long way in helping it stop.

Example methods:

- Pull groups together to talk about the incident.

- Open the door for communication. Speak with your employees and answer any questions employees may have.

- Hold weekly meetings to address any recent "word around the office". Address any concerns or problems employees may have. Also use this time to offer facts and information that can stop the gossip and alleviate any doubts or negativity.

## Do Not Participate

One of the best ways to end gossip or rumors is to simply not share it with others. Gossip feeds on those willing to send it down the grapevine and has trouble moving on when it hits a brick wall. Participating in the rumor mill not only perpetuates it, but you discredit and even belittle yourself. As a person in a management position, any participation in office gossip can portray you in a negative way and may you appear to be a non-team player.

## Deal With it Swiftly

Refusing to pass on a rumor or piece of gossip won't end its cycle through the office. When something like this approaches you, speak openly with the person who told it to you and let them know you don't intend to share the information with anyone else. Also tell them why you believe the information could be hurtful if passed along any further. This shows you will not participate in that kind of behavior and help shed some light for the other person to see how negative their actions are as well. Follow up with other employees and have the same discussion with them. If needed, have a meeting with the office and address a group of employees at once. The quicker these problems are approached, the sooner the grapevine will stop and work can continue.

# Chapter 3 – Office Personalities

Every employee is unique in their job skills and office presence. That also means every employee has their own office personality. While many are tolerable and even upbeat, some can have negative effects on other employees. Managers should understand these different types and know how to handle them in the workplace.

## Complainer

The complainer in the office is typically the employee who always finds something to complain about on the job, whether it includes the amount of hours they work, the assignments they get, or simply the type of coffee in the break room. They love to circulate bad news and feed off of the misery of others. They were most likely a model employee, but then probably had too many confrontations with coworkers or negative comments from upper management.

Tips when handling a complainer personality:

• Try to keep their views in perspective.

• Direct their negativity toward more positive views.

• Instead of listening to their opinions, form your own.

• Don't let their cynical views blur your vision of the office.

## Gossiper

The primary mission of the office gossiper is to know and share the latest scoop of the office; and if they don't know it, they'll simply make it up. They have a need to feel important and think that since they hold the key to the best information, this puts them on top. A gossip will purposely seek those who are willing to listen and feed on the attention. While they believe this type of behavior makes them more likable and popular, it can actually have the opposite effect, making them untrustworthy and undependable.

Tips when handling a gossiper personality:

• Avoid engaging in their gossip or rumors.

- State that you are not interested in what they may have to offer.

- Do not pass on information they may have passed onto you.

- Avoid discussing any personal matters near them, unless you want the entire office to know.

## Bully

There are several types of office bullies with several different characteristics, but their behavior is generally the same. Bullies look to dominate and control their work area. They often insult or downplay their coworkers or their performance in order to distract from theirs. Bullies have their own 'growl' that they use to make employees fear them and comply with what they say. Only when they feel like they have control and power will they feel happy.

Tips when handling a bully personality:

- Don't try to challenge them. This only feeds their bully persona.

- Don't take their remarks personally. Chances are it's really not about you.

- Avoid trying to please them. They can normally not be satisfied so easily.

- When addressing their behavior, do it privately and calmly.

## Negative Ned / Nancy

Negative Ned and Nancy typically do not trust anyone with authority or power. They have the "they're out to get me" attitude. While they believe that they are always right, they hold back on answers but are quick to let out ''told you so" when things go wrong. This personality always sees the down side of any situation.

Tips when handling a negative Ned/Nancy personality:

- Stay positive, but stay realistic.

- Avoid trying to simply find a solution since they will dismiss them.

- Stick with the facts.

- Avoid arguing with them or trying to correct them.

As we've stated, every employee is unique and brings his own personality to the office. Some of these personalities can have negative effects not only on fellow coworkers and management, but even the whole office. Here we discuss more personality types a manager could encounter and ways to handle them in the workplace.

**Information Keeper**

Information keepers are similar to know-it-alls, except that they tend to keep the information to themselves, rather than blasting it all over the office. Their power comes from within, in which they know the information needed and wait for others to seek them out. They thrive on gathering information on all subjects and departments, even if they are not an active part of it.

Tips when handling an information keeper personality:

- Realize it's alright to ask for their help, but don't let them control the situation.

- Don't try to correct them or get them to change their mind.

- Stick to the topic at hand – don't wander into other categories.

- Don't try to compete with them.

**Know-It-All**

The know-it-all is the person in the office that is very skilled in their area and makes a great expert on the subject, but makes a poor coworker. Whether you've asked for their help or not, they are more than willing to show off what they know and what they can do. Their arrogance can make them hard to work with, but their expertise is a key asset to the office.

Tips when handling a know-it-all personality:

- Keep them focused on the task or information needed.

- Don't be afraid to ask for their help, but keep it work related.

- Avoid trying to compete with them.

- Don't argue or correct them if something is incorrect. Offer to speak with them privately.

**The Apple - Polisher**

There are often many names for the apple-polisher type – such as boss's pet, brown-noser, or frankly just the office 'suck up'. Since they fear rejection, an apple polisher will be overly nice and polite to feel accepted. They love to give praise since they think it gets them ahead. They always volunteer for projects, even if it hasn't been asked yet. They usually put their relationship with the manager above their relationship with their peers, which can make then unlikable in the workplace. In extreme cases, the apple-polisher can become a 'snitch' if they feel it would put them on the good side of management.

Tips when handling an apple-polisher personality:

- Always speak with this person in private.

- Find what the employee really needs – not just what they are willing to take.

- Avoid giving flat out rejection.

- Thank them for their effort and willingness to help, but remind them they don't have to do it all to be a great team member.

**Nosey Neighbor**

The nosey neighbor type is the one in the office that always wants to know everyone else's business. They constantly ask personal questions and can appear in your office several times a day. While this employee can be annoying, they often believe they are just being helpful or even friendly. It is not easy to deflect this type of person since if they are not handled with care, they can intensify and try harder to become closer.

Tips when handling a nosey neighbor personality:

- Answer their prying questions with as few facts as needed.

- Remain friendly but don't feed into their need for information.

- Avoid talking about your personal life at work.

- When asked personal questions, try to shift their focus back to work related matters.

# Chapter 4 – Getting Support for Your Projects

Sometimes it can seem hard to gain support behind your office projects, but don't throw in the towel so early. Some of the key aspects of gaining support are building relationships with the staff, making allies that can give you a boost, and not being afraid to show others what you have to offer. Using honest and 'good' politics cannot only gain support for any project you may be carrying, but will propel your career forward without burning bridges behind you.

## Gain Trust Through Honesty

A manager that instills confidence and mutual trust creates an office environment that holds to high standards and clear ethics. Although office politics can make some people think of terms like deception and trickery. Keep in mind that honesty and trust will provide a more powerful and lasting benefit to the employee and propel their career further. Don't lie or cover up recent mistakes you might have made. Be open about steps you've had to take to correct situations. When asked for statistics or reports for your project, offer them freely. It's important to build trusting relationships that people can depend on to gain support over time. Relationships built on dishonesty and misguidances do not hold up.

Helpful tips:

- Be polite an honest with coworkers.

- Be open with others and don't be afraid to 'tell it like it is" rather than beat around the bush.

- Don't use deception and lies, or 'bad' politics to get ahead.

**Be Assertive**

Being assertive can often be misconstrued as being mean or just being a jerk. But belittling, intimidating or trying to control those that could very well help you will cause trouble in the office and will cause you to lose others' respect. Being assertive requires one to be confident without being aggressive. Don't be afraid to say what you want or need, and as long you do it tactfully and respectfully. If your answer is no, don't give up right away. Regroup and rethink what you need to do in order to go for your goal.

Helpful tips:

- Be confident, but not arrogant.

- Don't be afraid of rejection or criticism.

- State what you want or intend to gain. Don't beat around the bush or use smoke and mirrors.

## Blow Your Own Horn

One of the best ways to gain support for your cause is to let others know what you have accomplished or what you can bring to the table in the future. Be cautious of the fine line between blowing your horn and downright bragging or being boastful. When speaking with those who can potentially give the support you need, subtly add in some of your recent successes or a good comment made on your last evaluation. Once they see your value and potential, you will have more people on your side next time you present your case in a staff meeting. Keep your comments truthful and realistic. Be sure not to just make up great things to say – those that want to back you will most likely check their facts first.

## Make Allies

Don't underestimate the power and value of having allies not only in your department, but other departments as well. To win them over, take time to learn how you can help and contribute with your time. Staying on good terms with different department heads can put you right in the middle of the networking movement in the company, and allow you to tap into every department when needed. This also allows you to not only build credibility, but strong office alliances that will prove very helpful.

Helpful tips:

- Alliances are not built overnight. Be committed.

- Offer your time to help other departments and managers. If you want them to do it for you, be willing to do it for them.

- Don't underestimate the little guys. Many alliances start small.

# Chapter 5 – Conflict Resolution

While conflict is bound to happen in any office, managers are still responsible for creating a work environment that allows its employees to work comfortably together without fear or hostility. Cliques, disagreements, and plain arguments can develop which can affect the entire office. As a manager, it is your responsibility to identify these conflicts and make sure they are resolved as soon as possible.

**The Importance of Forgiveness**

Conflict causes stress and emotional pain. Once a conflict has been resolved, it is important to forgive all parties involved. Those who do not forgive can be caught in a circle of anger and resentment, affecting not only their work performance, but others as well. Forgiveness allows a person to let go of the blame and pain and feel the weight come off of their shoulders.

Forgiveness benefits:

- Enables one to feel more empathy toward the other party.

- Provides the parties to repair any damage to their relationship.

- Allows employee(s) to feel less like a victim and more of an active role in the resolution.

**Neutralizing Emotions**

When a manager attempts to ignore or push aside emotions in a conflict, it can not only make the original conflict worse, and it makes the manager part of the conflict as well. The negative emotions are soon pointed at the manager and can create more problems than intended. In any case, before a conflict can begin to be resolved, the manager must first neutralize the emotions. Once this is done, the problem can be looked at objectively and settled more calmly.

Tips on handling emotions:

- Remind the employee(s) of their positive attributes, which draws attention away from the negative emotions.

- Offer solutions you can personally provide, such a change in assignments, or a one-on-one meeting.

- Above all, acknowledge the parties' feelings. Some employees just want to be heard.

## The Benefits of a Resolution

Resolving a conflict can make any work environment feel powerful. Employees feel as though they can go on about their day rather than feel the stress of conflict and arguments. Although, conflict can never be eliminated from the office, employees and managers can learn how to manage conflict and keep these frustrating instances to a minimum.

Common benefits of resolving conflicts:

- Requires the employee(s) to take ownership in their own actions

- Allows people to listen to each other and consider different point of views.

- Enables employees to play a part in their own resolution, rather than being done completely by management.

## The Agreement Frame

The Agreement Frame is used to explain the employee's viewpoint during a conflict in a firm way, without offending the other party and without demeaning their own position. The Agreement Frame is meant to encourage open discussion and conversation between all parties involved.
Employees should start the conversation with "I agree…and…" I appreciate…and…", "I respect…and…", "I believe…and…" or even "I think…and…" These phrases allow the employee to acknowledge how the other party is feeling but also lets them interject with their own opinions as well. When used correctly, the Agreement Frame can be a great tool for resolving any conflict.

Remember:

- Allow both parties to speak and encourage using the previous key phrases.

- Make employees focus on what they want in the solution

- Using words such as "but", "although", "however", "nonetheless", etc. are negative adverbs and can distract from the final solution. Avoid using them while employees are speaking.

# Chapter 6 – Ethics

Ethics is a set of standards used to judge from right and wrong. In the workplace, it can refer to the act of fair competition, acting honestly and treating coworkers and management respectively. Every day managers will need to make ethical decisions that will affect their employees as well as themselves. That's why it is very important that the manager understands their company's ethical obligations so that they can not only meet the requirements set forth, but to also display appropriate behavior for their employees and coworkers.

**Benefits of an Ethical Environment**

An office that creates an ethical environment is an office where employees can feel safe and trusted. Employees that work in this type of environment are proven to work harder and increase productivity over time. When workers know they're management follows a code of ethics, they are more inclined to go above and beyond for them and excel in their work.

Additional benefits:

- Enables open communications between management and employees.

- Employees are more likely to report misconduct.

**Lead by Example**

Since good ethics are first noticed at the top, management must lead by example. Employees may sit through seminars or see a poster in the break room about good ethics, but they are truly learning ethics from the people that surround them, including management. So as a key tool in this learning process, it is important that, as a manager, you are up to speed on the company's code of ethics and how to carry them out.

Remember:

- Managers are to uphold the ethical standards for the entire company.

- Employees look to you for guidance. Give them an example worth following.

## Ensuring Ethical Behavior

Now that you are leading your employees by example in your ethical behavior, how do you ensure the ethical behavior in others? Many companies use various types of ways to first instill their ethics and then ensuring they are carried out, such as training programs or handbooks. Some use bribes and rewards that are given when good ethical behavior is seen. The opposite method is also used, in which employees are quickly disciplined when they display unethical behavior. This effect is normally done in a semi-private way to 'make an example' of the employee and discourages others from committing the same act or acts. Both methods should be used with caution, since they can actually *lead to* unethical behavior. As a manager, it is up to you as to how you can effectively ensure ethical behavior in your workplace.

Example methods:

- Reward programs

- Discipline plans

- Training sessions – including posters, handbooks and manuals

**Addressing Unethical Behavior**

Unethical behavior is never fun to catch. One of the main problems after witnessing such behavior is how to address it properly so that the behavior can be corrected. Employees can have a hard time exposing unethical behavior if it is not clearly defined or runs a risk or retaliation of some sort. Managers can face the same problems at times, so it is best for the company to create some sort of policy or procedure on how to report any witnessed behavior. With clear instructions outlined, employees and managers don't have to hesitate reporting the unethical behavior.

Key points to addressing the unethical behavior:

- Speak directly with the employee, preferably in private.

- Use empathy and understanding, but remain firm that the behavior was inappropriate.

- Adhere to the company policy and the consequences stated.

- Carry out such consequences and remind the employee (if still in your employ) that this type of behavior is unacceptable.

28

# Chapter 7 – You are Not an Island

Sometimes, as a manager, we can feel like we are on our own little island doing our job as intended. But don't forget to look up and see your team of employees that are there to work for and with you, as well as partners in upper management. No one can manage everything by themselves, and will need to reach out from time to time. Sometimes we find that we may need to reach out to those we've just met, or even someone we thought we'd left behind.

**Never Burn a Bridge**

Whether you left another company to come to this one or you are moving departments, there is always a bridge behind you that is moving you forward. Our natural instinct is to let out our frustrations on the people you no longer have to see, but burning that bridge behind you won't erase the past and could harm your future. You never know when or where you'll need to face the company or person again. You'll want to ensure if you do meet again or if you ever need their assistance (a reference perhaps), that you'll be in their favor.

Tips:

- Leave with notice, if possible.

- Do not leave in anger – keep all negative comments and frustrations to yourself.

- Thank the manager or HR for your time at the company. They will remember your gracious attitude when they are called for a reference.

**Take the High Road**

"Taking the high road" simply means to make a decision based on moral, or to act ethically. When faced with a difficult decision, the manager should 'take the high road' to either resolve the problem or correct what they might have done wrong. The key to doing this is to have certain boundaries and use them when needed. Acknowledge the position someone else may hold, even if you do not like it or agree with them, and then use your boundaries to express your side with being negative or unethical. Even if the situation is not any better, it certainly did not get worse.

Helpful tips:

- Take a deep breath and think about what *should* be done, rather than what is currently *being* done.

- Think about the kind of person you want to exhibit to those around you – show it in your actions.

- Remember that we all have disagreements and make mistakes. How would you want the other person to treat you in you were in their shoes?

### Trust is a Two-Way Street

Employees want to trust their manager and depend on them for their needs at work. It is important for the manager to build trust between themselves and their employees, especially since this may help repair any trust deficiencies made somewhere else. When managers show trust in their employees and believe in their hard work, employees will continue to strive to do well for their managers and show their trust in return.

Tips to help build trust:

- Show confidence in your employees.

- Be honest and tell the truth, even if it makes you look bad or puts you at a disadvantage.

- Demonstrate that your words are consistent with your actions – make due on your promises.

### Don't Hide in Your Office

Office employees count on their managers to be leaders and want to know that they are there to face tough office situation when they arise. Some managers try to find the benefit of staying in their office, perhaps to gain focus or ignore non-office related chatter, but in reality it is actually hurting the team they are trying to focus on. When the manager spends most of their time behind a closed door, employees begin to feel neglected and can start to resent their manager. Make it a point to come out of the office and speak with your employees and how they are doing on the job. Your employees will respect you more as a coworker and an ally then the stuffy manager that hides behind closed doors.

# Chapter 8 – Social Events Outside of Work

While socializing outside of work can generally sound like a great idea (the team that plays together stays together), there comes a time when employees and managers should respect each other's boundaries and know when to spend time apart. Also, employees and managers must spend some time away from the stress and hustle of the office and should not take their job with them when they go out.

**How to Decline Politely**

Managers can't, or don't want, to necessarily attend social events with their employees, whether it's because of the late nights, difference of interests or simply a lack of time. Even though there is nothing wrong with this, it is important to offer a polite decline rather than just giving your employees the cold shoulder. When asked to attend an event or gathering, thank the person for the invitation and simply state that you cannot attend for whatever reason. The employees may laugh or mock it a little at first, but they will grow to respect you and your reasoning. To avoid losing touch with them altogether, you can plan and offer your own events to invite your coworkers to that are more your style or that can fit into your schedule. It won't keep them from doing their own thing, but it does allow the chance for them to spend time with you and socialize outside of work.

Common reasons to decline a social event:

- Family responsibilities

- Lack of time/schedule permitting

- Lack or difference of interests

**Rules When Attending**

When a group from the office is planning to get together outside of the workplace setting, it is always best to instill a set of spoken or even unspoken boundaries. Things such as client information or personal employee information should not be brought to the table. If time permits, gather the group before and discuss what sort of boundaries need to be set, whether personal or professional.

Common rules and boundaries set:

- No talking about the office (client, salaries, assignments, coworkers).

- Pictures should be kept to a minimum and not posted on a social networking site without the subject permission.

- The event does not prevent the employee from coming to work the next day.

**Meeting New People**

When meeting new people outside of work, things can either feel natural or turn awkward real fast. Sometimes we're unsure of ourselves outside of work and are unsure of the identity we put out there. After all, out here you're not just the manager and coworker; you're Joe/Bob/Susan/Anne, etc.

Situations like these can go back to our grade school days and remember how you made new friends, plain and simple:

- Approach people calmly and say something about yourself. Ask them to return the favor.

- Keep introductions short. They don't need to know your entire resume in one conversation.

- If you encounter someone who is rude or being a jerk, smile politely and simply move on.

**Conversation Dos and Don'ts**

One of the general social event rules is to have an understood list of topics that should not be discussed when out with colleagues. As stated before, information such as company client list or employee salaries should rank high on the do not discuss list. Other topics can include employee evaluations or assignments, office meetings or even other coworkers. Some offices choose to just eliminate office talk altogether.

You can't control what employees talk about when they are out, but you can influence the conversation at the events you choose to attend. Let your group know what subjects are off limits or would be inappropriate. Clarify any misunderstandings before they have a chance to rise.

## Additional Titles

The 90 Minute Guide series of books covers a variety of general business skills and are intended to be completed in 90 minutes or less. It is an effective way for building your skill set and can be used to acquire professional development units needed by project managers and other industries to maintain their certification. For the availability of titles please see

https://www.silvercitypublications.com/shop/.

No. 1 - Appreciative Inquiry

No. 2 - Assertiveness and Self Control

No. 3 - Attention Management

No. 4 - Body Language Basics

No. 5 - Business Acumen

No. 6 - Business and Etiquette

No. 7 - Change Management

No. 8 - Coaching and Mentoring

No. 9 - Communications Strategies

No. 10 - Conflict Resolution

No. 11 - Creative Problem Solving

No. 12 - Delivering Constructive Criticism

No. 13 - Developing Creativity

No. 14 - Developing Emotional Intelligence

No. 15 - Developing Interpersonal Skills

No. 16 - Developing Social Intelligence

No. 17 - Employee Motivation

No. 18 - Facilitation Skills

No. 19 - Goal Setting and Getting Things Done

No. 20 - Knowledge Management Fundamentals

No. 21 - Leadership and Influence

No. 22 - Lean Process and Six Sigma Basics

No. 23 - Managing Anger

No. 24 - Meeting Management

No. 25 - Negotiation Skills

No. 26 - Networking Inside a Company

No. 27 - Networking Outside a Company

No. 28 - Office Politics for Managers

No. 29 - Organizational Skills

No. 30 - Performance Management

No. 31 - Presentation Skills

No. 32 - Public Speaking

No. 33 - Servant Leadership

www.ingramcontent.com/pod-product-compliance
Lightning Source LLC
Chambersburg PA
CBHW060704280326
41933CB00012B/2299